Copyrighted material

LAUGHING ON THE EDGE

The Uncensored Life and Legacy of Richard Pryor, A Journey Through Comedy and Tragedy

Tommy W. Pate

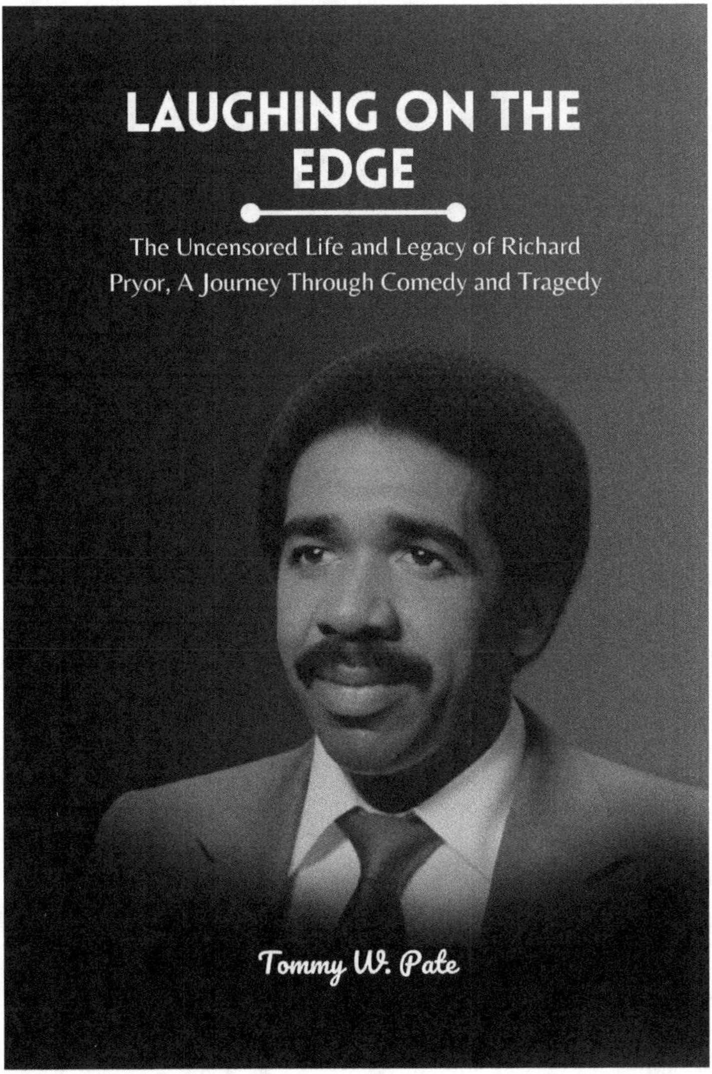

Laughing on the Edge

The Uncensored Life and Legacy of Richard Pryor, A Journey Through Comedy and Tragedy

By

Tommy W. Pate

Copyrighted material

All rights reserved. No part of this publication may be reproduced, distributed, or transmitted in any form or by any means, including photocopying, recording, or other electronic or mechanical methods, without the prior written permission of the publisher, except in the case of brief quotations embodied in critical reviews and certain other noncommercial uses permitted by copyright law.

Copyright © Tommy W. Pate, 2024.

Table of Contents

Preface..6
Introduction..9
Chapter 1..10
   Born to be a Fighter...10
   The Comedian's Ascent: Entering the Scene......... 15
   Early Records and Television Success................... 18
   Discovering His Voice: The Style Revolution..........20
Chapter 2..23
   Creative Methods for Telling Stories.......................23
   Hollywood Calling.. 29
   The Stand-Up Specials..33
   Internal Hells: Struggles with Dependency.............37
Chapter 3..43
   Political Commentary and Activism........................ 43
   Trials and Tribulations...47
   His Return to stage.. 52
Chapter 4..63
   Insights from Friends, Family, and Collaborators... 63
   Creative Collaborations... 71
   Pryor as a Pioneering Entrepreneur....................... 75
   Pryor's Cultural impact... 79
Chapter 5..84
   An Analytical Examination of Pryor's Most

Distinguished Performances............................84
Pryor's Narrative Method...........................87
Pryor's Legacy in Today's Comedy Scene..............92
Pryor's Influence on the Dramatic Arts...................97
Chapter 6.. 102
Relationships and Marital life of Richard Pryor.....102
Pryor as a Social Commentator............................106
The Last Draw..110
Moral and Life Lessons from the Story of Richard Pryor... 113

Preface

I was motivated to write this biography of Richard Pryor because I had a great deal of respect and admiration for his groundbreaking work and the lasting impact he had on American culture. Pryor was more than just a comedian; he was a social critic, a storyteller, and a cultural icon whose influence stretched beyond the realm of stand-up comedy to encompass the contemporary entertainment landscape.

My goal in delving into Pryor's personal and professional life was to paint a picture of the private man who struggled with his vulnerabilities and demons, in addition to the public figure recognized for his raw performances and incisive humor. His journey was one of contradictions and contrasts, spanning from his early years in a Peoria brothel to the pinnacles of Hollywood fame. His comedy reflected the harsh realities of his upbringing, but he also used laughter as a coping mechanism and a way to connect with others.

This book is based on interviews with friends, family, and collaborators who supported Pryor during different stages of his life, as well as a variety of sources that provide insight into his career pursuits and personal struggles. I hope that readers will gain a nuanced understanding of Pryor's character and the social challenges he faced from this insightful exploration of his career. It has been a journey in and of itself to write this biography; it has forced me to look past the laughter, the suffering, the victories, and the tribulations of a man who could make the whole world laugh while he was breaking inside. Richard Pryor leaves us with many memories, but his legacy also includes his fearless facing of life's darker sides, which makes him a figure worth researching and honoring long after his last curtain call.

As you peruse the pages of this book, I cordially welcome you to accompany me in discovering the life of a man whose contributions have transformed comedy forever and who, by sharing his weaknesses, helped every one of us understand our own a bit better.

Introduction

This book promises to paint a comprehensive portrait of a complex man whose humor and humanity touched millions. Whether you're a longtime fan or new to his legacy, get ready to be moved, entertained, and inspired by the life of Richard Pryor. Welcome to the fascinating journey of one of the most influential comedians of all time! Through candid anecdotes, personal reflections, and a vivid exploration of his professional achievements and personal trials, you will dive into the depths of Pryor's turbulent life, from his humble beginnings in Peoria, Illinois, to his ascent as a groundbreaking artist who redefined the landscape of comedy. Enjoy the journey!

Chapter 1

Born to be a Fighter

Early Years in Peoria, Illinois

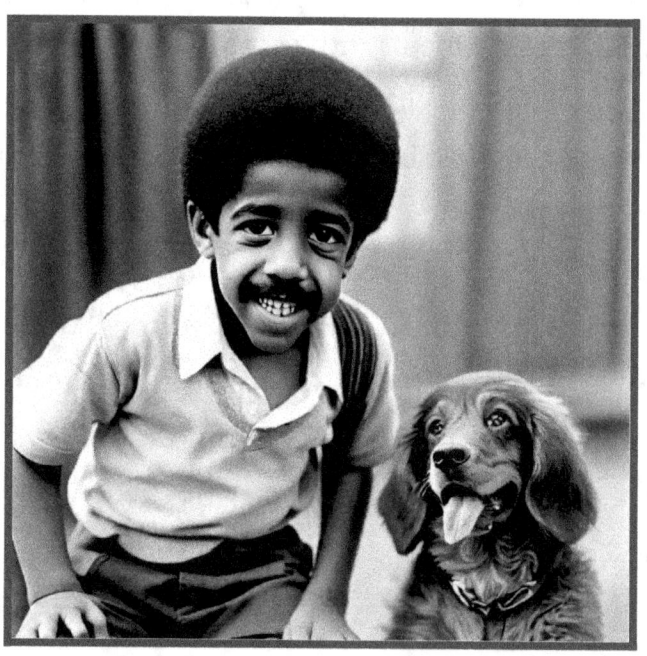

One of the most significant comedians in American history, Richard Pryor whose real name was Richard Franklin Lennox Thomas Pryor was born on December 1, 1940, in Peoria, Illinois. He was Born into a family with a poor background, a family with abject poverty. His early years in Peoria helped to shape the man he would become and the humor he would share with the world. He lived a life full of struggle and misfortune that he almost commit suicide while experiencing a lot of tribulation. In short, he had a miserable life during his upbringing in Peoria.

Infancy and Family History
Richard Pryor was raised in his grandmother's brothel, where his upbringing bestowed upon him a gritty, unfiltered view of human nature and interactions. Richard was born into an environment steeped in the harsh realities of the mid-20th-century African-American experience in the Midwest. As a child, he was exposed to a turbulent life in Peoria's red-light district of North Washington Street. His father, LeRoy "Buck

Carter" Pryor, was a boxer and bartender with a violent temper.

Education and Formative Impacts

After attending several public schools in Peoria, Pryor frequently talked about the influence of growing up in a violent and impoverished neighborhood and how these experiences influenced his comedy. Despite these difficult circumstances, he found an early love for acting, first through music and then comedy. He was first exposed to the world of storytelling and entertainment through movies and live shows in Peoria's local theaters, which sparked his interest in stand-up comedy. This simply tells us to have a dream and chase it, be enthusiastic about your dream, do not despair even in times of difficulties and hardship, success will surely come one day.

Creative Encounters

One of Pryor's most influential early experiences was performing at the Carver Community Center, a local community center. These early shows helped him refine his craft and provided a much-needed diversion from his otherwise chaotic life. Pryor learned to use humor to navigate his personal experiences, transforming difficult realities into material for comedy. His ability to make people laugh became a potent tool for both connection and catharsis.

Racist Encounters

Racism is *inevitable* in the journey of success, Pryor learned to use humor as a form of social commentary, addressing complex issues like race relations, social injustice, and personal identity. These themes would later become central to his act, distinguishing him as a comedian willing to confront and challenge societal norms. Growing up in the segregated America of the 1940s and 1950s,

Pryor's early encounters with racism had a profound impact on his comedic voice.

Traveling Out of Peoria

The harsh realities of Pryor's childhood and adolescence in Peoria, however, remained a cornerstone of his comedic and artistic expression, evident throughout his career. Determined to pursue an entertainment career, Pryor left Peoria in his late teens, a move that marked the end of his formative years and the beginning of his professional journey. He ventured to larger cities with more opportunities, initially struggling but gradually making a name for himself.

His Peoria Years' Legacy

Pryor's early years in Peoria, with all their complexity and contradiction, were not just a backdrop for his comedy, but the very substance of his artistic genius. His upbringing in Peoria gave him resilience and a unique perspective on life's absurdities, which he masterfully translated into comedy. His ability to blend humor with poignant social critique earned him a place in the hearts of audiences around the world.

Knowing Richard Pryor's Peoria, Illinois, roots helps one better appreciate how his early life influenced his topics and humorous style, changing the face of American comedy for all time.

The Comedian's Ascent: Entering the Scene

A story of talent, perseverance, and metamorphosis, Richard Pryor's rise from a struggling performer to one of the most iconic comedians in American history starts in the early 1960s, a time of social unrest and the emergence of a counterculture that Pryor would later help define with his distinct comedic voice.

Pryor moved away from Peoria and settled in several cities, including New York City, where he tried to establish himself in the competitive entertainment world. He started out doing stand-up comedy in small clubs, often playing to hostile crowds that weren't used to his unfiltered, uncooked material. These early appearances greatly influenced the way he performed and helped him learn the ins and outs of the genre.

Bill Cosby's relatively safe, non-confrontational humor shaped Pryor's early act, but he soon realized that this style did not fit him or the realities he wanted to explore; this realization was a turning point in his career, leading him to adopt a more provocative, introspective approach that would become his signature.

Innovation and Development

Following his move to Berkeley, California in 1963—a time of profound cultural and political upheaval—Pryor became embroiled in the counterculture movement and started experimenting with his material, incorporating themes of poverty, racism, and later his own experiences with addiction. His audacious, narrative-driven routines pushed the boundaries of comedy, making him a voice for both African American experiences and universal human truths.

Because of his connections to a community of writers, musicians, and artists in Berkeley, Pryor was able to use his platform not only for entertainment but also for commentary and critique, which helped his performances resonate with audiences of both black and white. His ability to communicate difficult social issues through humor and storytelling increased his appeal and profoundly affected society.

Early Records and Television Success

By the late 1960s, Pryor had started doing television appearances and recording several hit albums. His television debuts on programs such as "The Ed Sullivan Show" and "The Tonight Show" exposed him to a wider audience, but television's strict censorship sometimes reacted negatively to his raw approach. Still, Pryor's live recordings on albums helped him share his uncensored opinions, garnering him praise from critics and a growing fan following. During a period of tremendous racial tension in America, Pryor's commercially successful album "That Nigger's Crazy" (1974) received a Grammy for Best Comedy Recording. This album, along with others like "...Is It Something I Said?"(1975), cemented Pryor's status as a comic pioneer by showcasing his talent for addressing touchy themes with honesty and fun.

Movies and Widening Impact

Opportunities in other forms of entertainment, especially film, expanded along with Pryor's notoriety. His film career, which flourished in the 1970s, featured writing and acting roles; he co-wrote the ground-breaking comedy "Blazing Saddles" (1974) with Mel Brooks and starred in a run of hit movies that included "Silver Streak" (1976) and "Stir Crazy" (1980). Pryor's roles frequently addressed racial and social norms, taking themes from his stand-up routines into new domains.

The rise of Richard Pryor as a comedian was not just about his career; it was also about how he altered the course of American comedy. Pryor's legacy can be seen in the work of innumerable comedians and artists who credit him as a major influence, ranging from Eddie Murphy and Chris Rock to Dave Chappelle and beyond. His unabashed confrontation of social issues, his candid exploration of race, and his ability to turn personal pain into universal humor all helped to shape the comedy landscape in America. Richard Pryor continues to be a pivotal character in the history of American comedy because of his innovative energy and lasting influence, which is evidence of the ability of humor to provoke thought, criticism, and inspiration.

Discovering His Voice: The Style Revolution

Richard Pryor's rise to prominence as one of the most significant comedians of the 20th century can be attributed to his relentless pursuit of the truth, his inventive sense of humor, and his unmatched capacity to transform social and personal issues into gripping comedic moments. His quest to discover his voice is a reflection of his maturation as a person and his observations on racial, class, and American society.

His early work was greatly impacted by the mainstream comedy of the day, which valued a clean, non-confrontational approach as demonstrated by comedians such as Bill Cosby. Nevertheless, Pryor felt that this approach was constrictive and unsatisfying because it did not address the realities of his upbringing in a Peoria, Illinois, brothel or the widespread racial injustices that were prevalent in the United States at the time.

The pivotal moment for Pryor occurred during a 1967 performance in Las Vegas. He was unable to carry on performing material that did not align with his truth, so he walked off the stage halfway through his set. This crisis sparked a period of self-examination and experimentation that ultimately resulted in a radical change in his comedic style, as he started to incorporate unfiltered, raw narratives about his life, his struggles, and the social issues he saw into his routines.

Combining Comedy with Ugly Truths

Using humor and deep social commentary, Pryor's new style was revolutionary; audiences responded deeply to his honest and raw treatment of subjects like racism, inequality, addiction, and his own complex personal life. His routines made people think and feel, not just laugh. Pryor used his platform to highlight the absurdities of racism and the systemic injustices that African Americans faced, frequently using his own experiences to illustrate his points.

In a powerful exploration of racial identity and self-awareness, Pryor, for instance, vows never to use the word "nigger" in his comedy again after visiting Kenya and not hearing the term used once. This shows how his experiences have shaped his comedy and how he has grown as a comedian.

Chapter 2

Creative Methods for Telling Stories

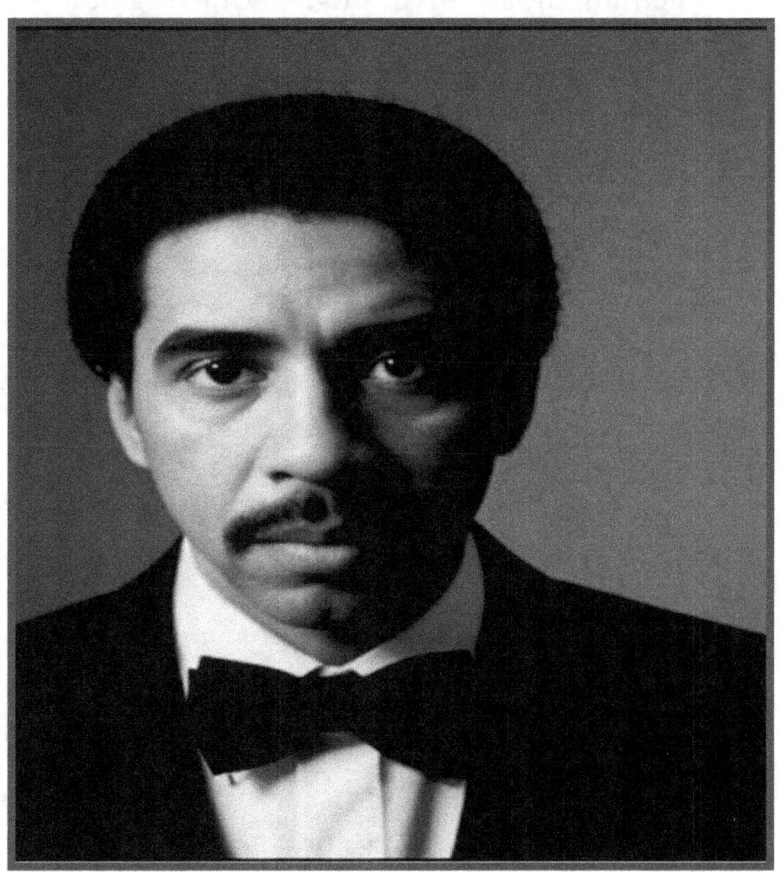

The capacity to create something novel and worthwhile is the hallmark of creativity, which is a complex and dynamic phenomenon. This "something" might be an original thinking or form, an idea, an artistic creation, a problem-solving strategy, or anything else that deviates from the status quo.

Creativity Aspects Include:

1. New and Novel: It needs originality or distinctiveness to be creative. Something that has never been seen or done precisely that manner before should be the end product.

2. Value: Something has to be significant, practical, or visually attractive in some way to qualify as creative. It should have a function, address an issue, provide comfort or understanding, or all three.

3. Divergent Thought: This is the capacity to come up with many original answers to a given issue. It stands in opposition to convergent thinking, which focuses on identifying a single, accurate solution to a problem.

4. Contextual Relevance: Creative products are often domain- or field-specific. Because it offers the fundamental abilities and comprehension required to create within a sector, domain knowledge is essential.

5. Detail-focused: Being creative involves more than simply the final product; it also involves the creative process. There are often phases of preparation, incubation, lighting, and verification in this process.

6. Associative Mindset: This is the capacity to see connections between apparently unconnected ideas or things. Creative minds can create new ideas or thoughts by connecting these various parts.

7. Taking Risks: There is always some danger involved with creative efforts. This might take the shape of experimenting with novel, unconventional methods or voicing opinions and ideas that contradict accepted wisdom.

8. Stability: Being creative often calls for commitment and tenacity. Working creatively might include a lot of revisions as well as overcoming a lot of obstacles and failures.

9. Intuition: Rather than logical, methodical reasoning, intuitive intuition is the source of many creative breakthroughs. The creative process may often be led in unexpected ways by this intuitive method.

10. Social and Cultural Factors: One cannot be creative in a vacuum. Cultural, social, and historical

settings have a big impact on it as they define what is important or innovative at any particular period.

Examining these many facets is necessary to comprehend creativity as they all play a part in the intricate process that results in the creation of original and significant concepts or goods.

In his comedy, Pryor frequently took on personas, bringing to life a variety of characters based on people he knew or imagined. These characters were not just caricatures; they were fully realized people who reflected broader societal truths. This approach not only provided entertainment but also offered astute insights into the human condition, turning his comedy into a form of social critique. Pryor's narrative style was characterized by vivid storytelling and character-driven humor.

Impact on Culture and Comedy

Comedians such as Eddie Murphy, Chris Rock, and Dave Chappelle have all cited Pryor as a major influence on their careers. Pryor's impact went beyond his stage appearances. He transformed the stand-up comedy scene by demonstrating that it could be a potent medium for social commentary and personal expression. His willingness to discuss taboo topics honestly and openly paved the way for future generations of comedians to explore similar themes in their work.

His legacy lives on in the innumerable comedians who follow in his footsteps, using humor as a tool for reflection, critique, and change. Richard Pryor's evolution of style was not just a personal victory; it was a cultural shift. He demonstrated the power of comedy to challenge and change societal norms and address painful truths in a way that was accessible and engaging.

A voyage of inner freedom and a dogged quest for truth, the metamorphosis of Pryor's comic style is a deep tale of discovering authenticity in art and sets a new benchmark for what comedy may achieve: making people laugh while making them think.

Hollywood Calling

A major turning point in Richard Pryor's career occurred when he made the leap from stand-up comedy to the big screen. Pryor's distinctive voice and viewpoint, which he brought to Hollywood, had a profound effect on how Black actors and characters were viewed and portrayed in mainstream American film.

While his early roles in films such as "Wild in the Streets" (1968) and "The Busy Body" (1967) gave him initial exposure, they did not fully convey the depth of his abilities; nonetheless, they were important stepping stones that helped him refine his skills in a new medium. Pryor turned his attention to Hollywood in the late 1960s and early 1970s, hoping to translate his comedic success into a motion picture.

Film Breakthrough

It was his performance in "Lady Sings the Blues" (1972), starring Diana Ross, that proved to be Pryor's real breakthrough in the film industry. The role proved to be a turning point in his Hollywood career, showcasing his versatility as an actor and earning him critical acclaim for handling more serious, dramatic material.

Pryor's rise to prominence in Hollywood allowed him to land major roles in movies that both made use of his comedic genius and provided social commentary. Movies like "Silver Streak" (1976), in which he starred opposite Gene Wilder, highlighted his comedic abilities and their on-screen chemistry became legendary, resulting in several more projects together, such as "Stir Crazy" (1980) and "See No Evil, Hear No Evil" (1989).

Impact on the Representation of African Americans

With his multi-dimensional and complex roles that offered a new narrative for Black characters in mainstream movies, Pryor's presence in Hollywood changed the way that African Americans were portrayed in movies. He also used his influence to directly address racial issues in his films, such as in "The Toy" (1982), where Pryor played a journalist who is "hired" as a toy for a wealthy White child, subtly criticizing the commodification of Black people in society.

Creative Direction and Input

He co-wrote the ground-breaking comedy "Blazing Saddles" (1974) with Mel Brooks, which parodied the racism of Hollywood's traditional Western genre; Pryor's creative input ensured that the film addressed racial issues with both humor and sharp critique, making it a critical and commercial success. By the mid-1970s, Pryor had gained significant influence in Hollywood, giving him more creative control over his projects.

Film Legacy

Richard Pryor's Hollywood career cleared the path for a new wave of African American comedians and actors by proving that Black entertainers could command large crowds and play a variety of roles in a wide range of genres. Pryor also broke down racial stereotypes in the business and made room for more complex and meaningful portrayals of African Americans.

Richard Pryor made a lasting impact on comedy and film with his pioneering spirit and unwavering commitment to being authentic in his roles. His move to the big screen was not only a career move but also a cultural turning point that changed the face of American film and carried on his legacy of breaking down barriers and questioning social norms.

The Stand-Up Specials

The history of stand-up comedy owes much to Richard Pryor's stand-up specials, especially "Richard Pryor: Live in Concert" (1979) and "Richard Pryor: Live on the Sunset Strip" (1982), which both reflected innovation and controversy. These specials not only highlighted Pryor's extraordinary comedic talent but also his willingness to take on social and personal issues, thereby raising the bar for what could be explored through comedy.

Unique Features of Pryor's Stand-Up Specials
Richard Pryor's Stand-up comedy was regarded as one of the best stand-up shows ever, "Richard Pryor: Live in Concert" was filmed at the Terrace Theatre in Long Beach, California. This

groundbreaking special was notable for several reasons: firstly, it was one of the first stand-up shows ever to be recorded and released as a feature-length film, which expanded the popularity and influence of stand-up comedy; secondly, Pryor's performance style in this special was particularly dynamic and expressive, using the entire stage and assuming multiple characters and voices to bring his stories to life; thirdly, his physicality and enthusiasm made the humor more relatable and powerful.

The subject matter of "Live in Concert" was groundbreaking as well; Pryor explored topics like racial tensions in society, police brutality, and the intricacies of his own life, including his turbulent upbringing and current experiences. His openness in talking about these subjects, along with his special talent for finding comedy in suffering, redefined stand-up comedy and had a lasting impact on subsequent comic generations.

A Comeback Special: "Live on the Sunset Strip"

After a nearly fatal freebasing accident in 1980 that drew intense media attention and public scrutiny, "Richard Pryor: Live on the Sunset Strip" was released. This special marked Pryor's comeback and he used the platform to confront his accident and recovery head-on, opening up about his addiction, his life-threatening burns, and his rehabilitation process in what was seen as a defiant act of self-reflection.

Shot at the Hollywood Palladium, "Live on the Sunset Strip" featured Pryor's reflections on his trip to Africa as well as his struggles; it carried on his tradition of fusing humor with commentary on race and identity. One particularly moving moment in the special was his discussion of how he decided to stop using the n-word after his trip to Africa, which highlighted his ongoing development as a comedian and a human being.

Disputes and Their Cultural Impact

Pryor used profanity and racial slurs to reclaim power and to reflect the realities of the African American experience, which was controversial but also seen as a form of artistic and social commentary. His raw, uncensored approach drew criticism from some quarters, who found his content offensive or too provocative, but it also earned him praise for his authenticity and courage. Both specials were controversial for their explicit language and the unapologetic way they dealt with sensitive and complex topics.

Beyond their immediate cultural impact, Pryor's stand-up specials altered the comedy landscape by showing that stand-up could be a vehicle for in-depth personal and societal analysis rather than just light entertainment. Pryor's skill at balancing comedy and tragedy, making audiences laugh and think at the same time, raised the bar for what comedians should be able to accomplish.

Conclusively, Pryor's innovative stand-up specials continue to be studied and revered for their innovative content and performance, underscoring his status as one of the most influential figures in the history of comedy. Pryor's groundbreaking stand-up specials left a lasting legacy that is evident in the way modern comedians approach their craft—combining personal narrative, social commentary, and raw honesty to engage with their audiences.

Internal Hells: Struggles with Dependency

As groundbreaking as his comedy, Richard Pryor's openness about his drug addiction provided a raw and frequently agonizing window into the intricacies of his life. His battles with drug addiction were a major source of inspiration for his comedic genius and also put his career and well-being in jeopardy. Pryor's issues with addiction began in the early years of his success. As he gained fame and financial resources, his exposure to the Hollywood party scene and its accompanying pressures and temptations increased. Pryor's drug of choice was cocaine, a substance that was both a stimulant for his creativity and a peril to his health. His addiction escalated during the 1970s and 1980s, a period that coincided with his rise to stardom.

His drug use had a dual effect on his career. On one hand, the uninhibited state it often induced helped fuel the raw, unscripted, and passionate performances that became his signature. His ability to transform personal pain into comedic material endeared him to audiences who found his honesty refreshing and relatable. However, his dependency also led to numerous professional setbacks, including missed performances, erratic behavior on set, and strained relationships with collaborators.

The Freebasing Incident
The most infamous episode in Pryor's battle with addiction occurred in 1980 when he set himself on fire while freebasing cocaine, an incident that nearly cost him his life. Pryor suffered severe burns over much of his body and underwent a lengthy and painful recovery process. Remarkably, he incorporated this near-death experience into his comedy, particularly in his stand-up special "Richard Pryor: Live on the Sunset Strip," where he addressed the incident with a mix of humor and stark honesty. This ability to use his personal struggles as material not only defined his style but also highlighted his extraordinary resilience.

Pryor's addiction led to several legal issues, including arrests and charges related to drug possession and tax evasion. These problems not only affected his public image but also his personal life, contributing to financial strain and multiple divorces. His health was severely compromised by his drug use, which contributed to a heart attack in the late 1970s and ongoing cardiovascular problems.

Reflection and Recovery

Following his critical freebasing incident, Pryor spent time in recovery, both physically from his burns and from his addiction. His subsequent work, particularly in "Live on the Sunset Strip," reflected a more introspective and mature outlook. He spoke candidly about his addiction, the pain it caused, and his journey towards sobriety. This period of reflection was crucial not only for his personal health but for his professional resurgence as he returned to film and television with renewed vigor.

Pryor's battles with addiction shaped his legacy in profound ways. By openly addressing his struggles, he broke taboos about discussing such issues in public, particularly in the African American community. His willingness to share these experiences made him a figure of both empathy and caution, illustrating the destructive potential of addiction as well as the possibility of redemption. His influence extends into the realms of how celebrities handle public revelations of personal struggles, paving the way for future artists to speak openly about their battles with addiction. His candid approach helped humanize him and made his comedy resonate on a deeper emotional level.

In summary, Richard Pryor's personal demons, especially his battles with addiction, deeply influenced his life and work. His struggle provided material for his art, which he wielded with unmatched skill, turning pain into laughter, and in doing so, offered a poignant commentary on human frailty and resilience.

Chapter 3

Political Commentary and Activism

Richard Pryor was not just a comedian; he was a profound social commentator whose work frequently intersected with the political landscape of his time. Through his comedy, Pryor explored and critiqued various aspects of American society, including race relations, systemic injustice, and the political climate. His unique voice in the realm of political commentary and activism left a lasting impact on social discourse.

His approach to comedy was deeply rooted in his observations of the world around him. He used his platform to address serious societal issues, often commenting on the absurdities of racism, the struggles of the working class, and the failures of political leadership. His stand-up routines and appearances often featured incisive commentary on the civil rights movement, police brutality, and institutional racism.

One of Pryor's most potent political tools was satire. He had a unique ability to use humor as a lens to critique society and politics, making complex issues accessible and relatable to his audience. For example, in his skits like "Little Feets" from the album *That Nigger's Crazy*Pryor used a fictional narrative to satire the historical oppression of African Americans and the ongoing civil rights struggles.

Activism and Advocacy

Beyond his performances, Pryor was actively involved in various causes and used his celebrity status to advocate for change. He was vocal about the injustices he witnessed and experienced, and he often participated in benefit performances to support civil rights organizations and other groups working towards social change.

Pryor's trip to Africa in 1979 had a profound impact on his personal life and professional outlook. After visiting Kenya and experiencing a society where Black people were in the majority and not subjected to the racial prejudices prevalent in the United States, Pryor returned with a renewed sense of identity and purpose. This experience led him to publicly renounce the use of the n-word in his routines, a significant decision that influenced other comedians and performers in addressing racial issues.

Influence on Social Discourse

Pryor's impact on social discourse was multifaceted. Through his stand-up, he offered a narrative that was both a reflection and a critique of American society. His unflinching honesty and willingness to address taboo topics helped to shift public conversations about race, poverty, and justice. He inspired a generation of comedians and artists to use their work as a form of social commentary.

Moreover, Pryor's influence extended into popular culture through his films and television appearances, where he continued to address political themes. In movies like *The Toy* and *Brewster's Millions*Pryor used humor to critique economic disparities and the commodification of Black lives in a capitalist society. His work in these films made poignant social statements while still delivering the entertainment value expected from a Hollywood production.

Legacy of Political Engagement
Richard Pryor's legacy as a political commentator is characterized by his ability to blend humor with hard-hitting social critique. He paved the way for other entertainers to address political and social issues openly, fostering a culture where comedians like Dave Chappelle, Chris Rock, and others

continue to influence political thought through their work.

Pryor's voice was one of fire — fiery humor, fiery passion, and fiery activism. His ability to ignite discussions on politically charged topics through comedy remains an enduring part of his legacy, demonstrating the power of comedy not just to entertain, but to challenge and inspire change. His work is a testament to the role of artists as agents of social transformation, using their talents to highlight injustices and advocate for a better world.

Trials and Tribulations

Legal and Health Battles

Richard Pryor's life was marked not only by groundbreaking success but also by significant personal struggles, including legal issues, tumultuous relationships, and severe health challenges. These aspects of his life, fraught with difficulty and adversity, shaped his public persona and influenced his work, giving depth to his comedy and his character.

Difficulties Faced

Throughout his career, Pryor faced several legal battles that stemmed from various incidents. His addiction to drugs often landed him on the wrong side of the law. For instance, in 1978, Pryor was arrested for tax evasion, which was a direct consequence of years of erratic behavior and financial mismanagement exacerbated by his drug use. Additionally, his drug addiction led to numerous run-ins with the police, including charges related to drug possession and assault. These legal issues were frequently covered by the media, affecting his public image and at times, his professional opportunities.

Multiple Marriages and Relationships

Pryor's personal life was equally turbulent, marked by multiple marriages and complex relationships. He was married seven times to five different women. These relationships were often volatile and made headlines, contributing to his public persona. His marriages were interspersed with other romantic liaisons, some of which were highly publicized due to their tumultuous nature. The instability in his personal life often mirrored the chaos of his professional life, where his groundbreaking comedy was born out of personal pain and complexity.

Severe Health Challenges

The most significant and life-altering of Pryor's struggles were his health issues. His lifestyle, marked by severe drug use, had long-term effects on his health, leading to a heart attack in 1977. However, the most devastating health challenge came in 1986 when Pryor was diagnosed with multiple sclerosis

(MS), a degenerative disease that affects the brain and spinal cord. This diagnosis came after years of experiencing a variety of symptoms, which he initially did not understand.

Multiple sclerosis affected Pryor profoundly; it gradually eroded his motor skills, leading to difficulties with movement, severe pain, and ultimately, a significant decline in his ability to perform. Despite these challenges, Pryor continued to make public appearances and perform stand-up, although his condition necessitated adjustments to his performance style and the venues in which he performed.

Impact of Health on His Career and Legacy
The onset of MS forced Pryor to shift the focus and style of his comedy. He incorporated his struggles with the disease into his act, using humor to cope with the pain and limitations imposed by MS. This move was in keeping with his lifelong approach to

comedy—translating personal pain into a shared experience that was both therapeutic and enlightening for his audience.

As his disease progressed, Pryor used a wheelchair and his speech became noticeably impacted. However, his mind remained sharp, and his ability to connect with an audience endured. His bravery in the face of such a debilitating illness only added to his legacy as not just a comedian, but a symbol of resilience.

Reflection

Richard Pryor's trials and tribulations, including his legal woes, tumultuous personal relationships, and his battle with multiple sclerosis, paint a portrait of a man who faced considerable adversity throughout his life. These challenges were interwoven with his career, influencing his comedy and public persona in profound ways. Despite these struggles, or perhaps because of them, Pryor's work resonated deeply with audiences, making him a beloved and influential figure in the world of comedy and beyond. His legacy as a trailblazer in tackling difficult personal and societal issues with humor and courage continues to inspire and impact artists around the world.

His Return to stage

Richard Pryor's career was marked by remarkable resilience in the face of numerous setbacks, including severe health issues and personal challenges. His attempt to revive his career, particularly after being diagnosed with multiple sclerosis (MS) in 1986, demonstrated his enduring spirit and commitment to his craft.

Return to Stand-Up Comedy

After his diagnosis, Pryor's health progressively worsened, but he continued to perform stand-up, adapting his style to accommodate his physical limitations. Despite the debilitating effects of MS, which often left him physically weakened, Pryor made several notable returns to the stage in the late 1980s and 1990s. These performances were characterized by his trademark humor, albeit delivered from a seated position or even from his wheelchair as his condition advanced.

One of the most significant aspects of Pryor's comeback was his ability to reflect on his life and earlier work with a mixture of humor and poignancy. His stand-up routines began to incorporate more introspective content, discussing not only his health struggles but also his reflections on his tumultuous life, including his battles with addiction, his multiple marriages, and the realities of aging.

Special Performances and Appearances

Pryor's comeback included several notable appearances that highlighted his ongoing influence in the world of comedy and beyond. He appeared in a few films and television shows during the 1990s, though less frequently than in the peak of his career. His movie roles during this period were often cameo appearances, as his health limited his ability to take on more demanding parts.

In 1993, Pryor made a memorable appearance on the television show "Saturday Night Live," hosted by his friend and fellow comedian Robin Williams. This appearance was significant as it showcased Pryor's undiminished ability to connect with an audience, despite his physical constraints.

Richard Pryor's life and work during his comeback phase were also the subject of several documentaries, which helped to cement his legacy and influence. These projects provided him an opportunity to reflect on his career and the impact of his groundbreaking style of comedy. Pryor participated in interviews where he spoke candidly about his successes and failures, his evolution as a comedian, and the ways in which his life experiences shaped his work. One of the most poignant reflections on his career came with the release of his autobiography, "Pryor Convictions and Other Life Sentences" (1995). The book offered an unflinching look at Pryor's life, from his early days in Peoria, Illinois, to his ascension as a comedy superstar, and his struggles with health and personal demons. It was both a critical and commercial success, providing fans and critics alike with deep insights into the complexities of his life and art.

Legacy and Influence

The latter part of Pryor's career and his attempts at a comeback highlighted not only his personal resilience but also the enduring appeal of his comedy. Despite the physical limitations imposed by his illness, Pryor continued to influence the comedy world. His ability to adapt his performance style and openly discuss his health issues broke new ground in how entertainers dealt with personal challenges.

Richard Pryor's return to the stage after overcoming such significant setbacks is a testament to his enduring spirit and his lasting impact on the world of entertainment. His life and work continue to inspire comedians and artists to tackle difficult personal and societal issues with courage and humor. His comeback, therefore, is not just a story of personal triumph but also a significant chapter in the history of American comedy, reflecting the power of resilience and the enduring nature of true artistic genius.

Examples of most funny jokes cracked by Richard Pryor

Richard Pryor, one of the greatest American stand-up comedians, was renowned for his ability to blend humor with hard-hitting social commentary. Pryor's jokes often tackled issues of race, personal struggles, and societal norms, all while maintaining a sharp sense of humor that resonated with a wide audience. Below are some examples of his humor that highlight his unique ability to make people laugh while also making them think.

1. On Race and Identity: Pryor's stand-up routines often delved into the complexities of race in America. One of his famous lines comes from a bit about his experience visiting Africa. After observing the diverse cultures and peoples, he joked, "I went to Zimbabwe... I know how white people feel in America now; relaxed! Cause when I heard the police car, I knew they weren't coming after me!" This joke, while humorous, underscored his reflections on racial profiling in the U.S.

2. Self-Deprecating Humor: Pryor was known for his vulnerability in his comedy, often using his own life as material. In one of his routines, he talks about setting himself on fire while freebasing cocaine, a public low point in his life. He turned this tragic event into a comedic story, saying, "Fire is inspirational. They should use it in the Olympics, because I ran the 100 meters in 4.3 seconds." Pryor's ability to laugh at himself endeared him to his audience, showing his resilience and humanity.

3. On Relationships: His observations on relationships often included sharp and witty insights. In one bit, he described the differences in how men and women argue: "You ever notice how men always win the argument when the women ain't around? They were like, 'And then I told my wife, listen here...' But when she's there, it's like, 'You're right, baby, I was wrong'." This joke highlights the universal nature of relationship dynamics, making it both relatable and funny.

4. On Children and Parenting: He also made light of parenting struggles, joking about how children could be manipulative. Pryor said, "I asked my kid, 'What do you want for Christmas?' He said, 'A world without war.' His method of asking for stuff—clever, making me look bad if I don't get it!" This kind of joke not only got laughs but also subtly critiqued societal issues through the innocent wishes of a child.

5. On Everyday Observations: Pryor's keen observational humor shone through when he talked about everyday situations. In one routine, he quipped about health food in the 1970s, "I went to a health food store, you know? I've been eating natural foods for three weeks and nothing happened. But I tell you this, I passed something that looked like a sneaker... and I've never eaten a sneaker." His way of exaggerating the mundane into the absurd highlighted his comedic genius.

6. On Everyday Racism: Pryor's ability to address systemic issues through his comedy was profoundly impactful. He often shared experiences of everyday racism with a mix of humor and poignant observation. One such example is when he joked about police encounters, "I went to jail for income tax evasion. I didn't know I was gonna go, though. I thought, 'You gotta go to court first.' And I figured I'd get a warning like they do when you run a stop sign." This joke not only made people laugh but also subtly critiqued the inconsistencies in legal enforcement based on race.

7. On Animal Encounters: Another recurring theme in Pryor's stand-up was his humorous tales involving animals, which often served to highlight human follies. He recounted a story about a monkey in a hotel room, saying, "The monkey took one look at me and jumped straight to the window, grabbed his little nuts, and said, 'Do you mind if I open this window?' Animals know who to mess with." This joke not only gets laughs for its absurdity but also cleverly comments on our interactions with nature.

8. On Hospital Experiences: Richard Pryor also mined his extensive hospital stays for humor. After suffering a severe heart attack, he described his medical treatment in his typically irreverent style: "The food they serve you in hospitals is enough to make you sick. If it wasn't for my condition, I'd have got up and left." His ability to find humor even in grim situations helped others to see the lighter side of life's darker moments.

9. Confronting Social Taboos: Pryor never shied away from discussing topics that were considered taboo. His routines often included candid discussions about sex, drugs, and other adult themes, delivered in a way that was both shocking and hilariously funny. He famously said, "I believe in the institution of marriage, and I intend to keep trying until I get it right," poking fun at his multiple marriages and divorces while also commenting on the complexity of intimate relationships.

10. Political Commentary: Even in the realm of politics, Pryor's wit was sharp. He often poked fun at political figures and their policies, highlighting the absurdity of political discourse. He joked, "You know there's a problem when the president starts running, not jogging. That means there's something we don't know about." This joke, while light-hearted, invited his audience to think critically about political transparency.

Through these examples, it's clear that Richard Pryor's comedy was much more than just making people laugh; it was about making them think. His legacy as a comedian who could artfully weave critical social commentary into his humor continues to influence comedians and entertain audiences worldwide.

Chapter 4

Insights from Friends, Family, and Collaborators

This is a comprehensive exploration into the life of the late Richard Pryor, offering a multifaceted view of one of the most influential comedians of the 20th century. This section is crafted from personal anecdotes and reflections provided by those who were closest to Pryor—friends, family members, and collaborators. These narratives serve not only to showcase Pryor as the iconic public figure he was but also to give a deeper understanding of his complexities as a private individual.

1.) Personal Anecdotes: The personal anecdotes shared in this section bring to light the many facets of Pryor's personality that were shielded from the public eye. For instance, his daughter Rain Pryor speaks about her father's softer side, which was rarely seen on stage. She recalls moments of quiet reflection Pryor had at home, his love for jazz music, and his unpublicized charitable acts that spoke volumes about his compassion and empathy towards others. Friends like Paul Mooney, a fellow comedian and writer, share stories of their time together on the comedy circuit, providing insights into Pryor's creative process and his relentless pursuit of authenticity in his work. Mooney highlights Pryor's ability to turn personal tragedy into comedic material, a quality that not only defined his career but also helped his audience connect with him on a profound level.

2.) Professional Reflections: Collaborators from various stages of Pryor's career, including directors like Sidney Poitier and actors he worked with, such as Gene Wilder, contribute their perspectives on working with Pryor. They discuss his approach to comedy and acting, his influence on the set, and how his fearless honesty brought a unique energy to every project. Wilder, in particular, recounts their dynamic in films like "Silver Streak" and "Stir Crazy," where Pryor's improvisational skills often brought new dimensions to their characters' relationships.

3.) **Family Insights:** Family members provide a look into Pryor's struggles and vulnerabilities, particularly with his battles against addiction and his health challenges. His wife Jennifer Lee Pryor discusses the complexities of their relationship, including the ways in which Pryor's fame impacted their personal life. She shares poignant memories of their times together, both good and bad, highlighting the human aspects of Pryor that were often overshadowed by his celebrity status.

Overall, Insights from Friends, Family, and Collaborators offers an intimate look at Richard Pryor, painting a portrait of a man who was as complex as he was talented. It delves beyond the public persona to reveal a person who faced numerous personal demons but always strove to bring laughter and joy to others. This section not only celebrates his genius but also humanizes him, presenting him as a man who loved deeply, fought bravely, and lived passionately. Through these diverse reflections, readers gain a rounded understanding of Pryor's life and work, both enriching and complicating his legacy as one of the greats in comedy.

Pryor and Racial Dynamics in America

In the aspect of racial abuse, this is a pivotal section that examines how Richard Pryor's comedy not only addressed but also challenged and transcended racial boundaries in America. Through his groundbreaking stand-up routines and cinematic endeavors, Pryor created a platform that fostered dialogue and provoked thought about race relations in the United States, making significant contributions to the cultural landscape.

Pioneering Racial Commentary in Comedy
Richard Pryor's approach to comedy was revolutionary, particularly in how he used his platform to explore and expose the intricacies of race and racism in America. His stand-up performances often delved into issues of race with a raw and unfiltered honesty that was rare at the time. Pryor's ability to discuss these themes openly on stage challenged both white and Black audiences, compelling them to confront uncomfortable truths about society's racial prejudices and inequalities.

One of the most significant aspects of Pryor's comedy was his use of language, especially his reclamation and use of racial epithets. This bold move was controversial but underscored his message about the power dynamics embedded in language. His routine "Niggers vs. Police," for example, highlighted the systemic racism within the police force, using humor as a tool to underscore a serious and dangerous reality for African Americans.

Pryor's Influence on Film and Television

Pryor's influence extended beyond stand-up comedy into his work in film and television, where he continued to push societal boundaries. In movies like "Silver Streak" and "Stir Crazy," Pryor played characters that, while comedic, also subtly confronted racial stereotypes and discrimination. His roles often flipped conventional racial scripts, placing a Black character at the center of narratives traditionally dominated by white characters.

Furthermore, Pryor's screenplays, such as the one for "Blazing Saddles" which he co-wrote but did not star in, included sharp racial satire that forced audiences to rethink their perspectives on race and racism. His contributions to the script helped cement the film as a critical piece of American cinema that used humor to challenge racial norms and prejudices.

Dialogue and Impact on Society

His comedy opened up new dialogues about race in America. By making his audiences laugh at the absurdities of racial discrimination, Pryor helped create a common ground where people could engage in conversations about race more openly. His impact was profound, as it allowed other comedians and artists to tackle similar issues in their work, helping to gradually shift public perception and foster a more critical understanding of race relations.

Legacy and Continuing Influence

The legacy of Richard Pryor's work in tackling racial issues continues to resonate today. Modern comedians and performers cite Pryor as a major influence in how they approach topics of race and identity in their own work. Shows and stand-up routines that address racial issues often draw on strategies that Pryor pioneered, using humor to provoke thought and encourage change.

In summary, we have been able to highlight how Richard Pryor was not just a comedian but a cultural force who used his platform to challenge and change the way race is discussed and perceived in the United States. Through his fearless approach to comedy and his unapologetic confrontation of racial issues, Pryor left an indelible mark on American culture, making him one of the most important figures in the history of comedy. His work opened doors for discussions about race that might not have been possible otherwise, setting a precedent for how artists can address social issues through performance and art.

Creative Collaborations

Partnerships that Defined a Career

In this section, we'll provide an insightful examination of how Richard Pryor's career was significantly shaped by his relationships with a range of collaborators across different media. From stand-up comedy to cinema, and from writing partnerships to musical engagements, Pryor's collaborations were instrumental in both honing his comedic style and pushing the boundaries of his creative expression. Listed below are some of his creative collaborations to mention a few;

1.) Comedy Partnerships: One of Richard Pryor's most significant and influential partnerships was with fellow comedian and writer Paul Mooney. Mooney was instrumental in helping Pryor develop his voice, crafting routines that pushed social boundaries and tackled complex issues such as race, identity, and societal norms. Their work together on Pryor's comedy albums and television specials, including the groundbreaking *The Richard Pryor Show*, showcased a synergy that was pivotal in the evolution of Pryor's comedic style, turning it into a powerful tool for commentary on social justice.

2.) Cinematic Collaborations: In the realm of cinema, Pryor's collaborations with actor Gene Wilder are legendary. The duo starred in several films that became classics, such as *Silver Streak*, *Stir Crazy*, and *See No Evil, Hear No Evil*. Their on-screen chemistry bridged racial divides and appealed to a wide audience, setting new standards for the portrayal of interracial friendships in Hollywood films. Their movies not only delivered laughs but also subtly challenged racial stereotypes and societal expectations. Pryor also worked closely with director Sidney Poitier in the comedy *Uptown Saturday Night*, where Poitier directed Pryor in a role that allowed him to explore a different facet of his acting ability. This collaboration was important as it paired Pryor with one of the first major African American directors in Hollywood, furthering the representation of African Americans in the film industry at multiple levels.

3.) Writing and Production: Behind the scenes, Pryor collaborated extensively with a variety of writers and producers. He co-wrote the groundbreaking film *Blazing Saddles* with Mel Brooks, though he was famously unable to star in the film due to contractual issues. His input helped shape the film's sharp satirical edge, particularly its bold commentary on race and the myth of the American West. In his later years, Pryor partnered with his wife Jennifer Lee Pryor, who played a crucial role in managing his career and later his legacy. Jennifer helped produce some of Pryor's more introspective and revealing work, including his stand-up performances chronicling his diagnosis with multiple sclerosis, showcasing a more vulnerable side of the comedian.

4.) Musical Endeavors: Pryor's collaborations were not limited to visual media; he also ventured into music. His partnership with soul and funk musicians like Curtis Mayfield, who composed the soundtrack for *Super Fly*, and his work with Quincy Jones, showcased Pryor's versatility and his ability to cross over into different artistic domains. These collaborations enriched his performances and brought a unique rhythm to his comedy, influencing the cadence and delivery that became trademarks of his style.

In summary, this exploration of Richard Pryor's collaborations reveals a man who was deeply interconnected with the creative world around him, drawing on the strengths of others to amplify his own voice and vision, ultimately leaving an indelible mark on the landscape of American culture.

Pryor as a Pioneering Entrepreneur

We will explore Richard Pryor's astute observation of the entertainment sector and his pioneering position in the comedy industry's business side in this part. In addition to being a brilliant comedian, Pryor was a shrewd businessman who understood early on how important it was to limit his artistic output and optimize his profits. This section examines his business ventures, his influence on comedic economics, and how he created new standards for actor independence and financial success in the entertainment sector.

Financial Independence and an Early Career

Richard Pryor learned early in his career how important it is to have both creative and financial control. Defying the conventions that a lot of comedians at the time followed, Pryor started making his comedy specials and albums. By making this decision, he was able to keep a larger portion of the earnings that would have otherwise gone to producers and promoters. His early comedic records, such as "That Nigger's Crazy," were essential to building his career and showcasing his singular ability to captivate listeners with his thought-provoking approach. These CDs not only established his humorous voice but also his standing as an accomplished independent artist in the field.

Making Agreements and Establishing Criteria
Pryor was able to negotiate terms that were unheard of for comedians at the time because he knew his market worth. He often negotiated beneficial terms into his contracts for comedy specials and movie roles, establishing a precedent for future deals that benefit both actors and comedians. When he negotiated an unprecedented $4 million movie contract with Columbia Pictures for three films in the late 1970s, for example, he set new standards for humorous actor salaries.

Pryor's Impact on Marketing and Distribution

One of the first comedians to realize the value of distribution, Pryor used a variety of outlets to reach his audience. His following and impact grew as a result of his stand-up specials being among the first to be extensively disseminated on emerging cable television networks. Pryor's performances were also able to reach a wider audience because of his clever use of the newly emerging home video market in the early 1980s, which brought in a sizable sum of money and cemented his legacy in the entertainment industry.

Production and Creative Control

One of the most important steps Pryor took to take back control of the creative parts of his work was to start his production firm. In addition to producing his concert videos, his production firm, Indigo Productions, gave him the freedom to work independently on TV shows and motion pictures that reflected his creative vision. For Pryor, retaining this control was essential because it guaranteed that his frequently contentious and provocative material would be presented in its truest form, preserving the integrity of his creative expression.

The Legacy and Its Effect on Upcoming Generations

Within the comedy community, Richard Pryor's commercial acumen and spirit of entrepreneurship have left a lasting impact. He taught comics of later generations the value of maintaining creative and financial control over their work. In Pryor's wake, comedians such as Eddie Murphy, Chris Rock, and Dave Chappelle have established their own production companies to maintain creative control over their work and negotiate better agreements.

Final Thoughts

It is clear that Richard Pryor was more than simply a comedian; he was a visionary businessman who radically altered the entertainment sector. His methodical approach to business, distribution, production, and negotiations made comedians more than just entertainers; they became important characters in culture and commerce. Pryor's lasting impact on the comedy industry is evidence of his forward-thinking methods, which shaped industry norms and gave performers the confidence to steer their careers.

Pryor's Cultural impact

The far-reaching influence of Richard Pryor on the American entertainment industry as a whole can never be overlooked, therefore cementing his place in history. His impact extended beyond stand-up comedy to include pop culture in general, music, cinema, and television. His distinct voice, daring approach to forbidden themes, and deep understanding of social concerns transformed the entertainment business and permanently altered American society.

Richard Pryor's cutting-edge, excruciatingly honest humor that touched on racial issues, daily life, and society transformed stand-up comedy. His unvarnished approach and talent for using humor to convey real stories inspired a new generation of comics, including Eddie Murphy, Chris Rock, Dave Chappelle, and Kevin Hart. These comedians credit Pryor as a mentor in navigating the challenges of celebrity and craft, in addition to being a significant influence on their comic approaches. Pryor's stand-up routines, which combined humor, realism, and empathy, redefined the way comedy could address societal challenges and personal suffering.

Effect on Cinema and Television
Pryor's impact went beyond the theater because of his work in movies and television. In several cinematic appearances, he gave his characters additional dimensions and often infused comic

insight into movies that also made social commentary. His portrayals of comedy mixed with strong, honorable characters in films like "Silver Streak," "Stir Crazy," and "Harlem Nights" set new standards for African American performers.

In addition, Pryor's short but significant television career with "The Richard Pryor Show" gave other African American actors and comedians a stage on which to display their skills. Even though the program had a brief run, its avant-garde treatment of humor, race, and social conventions had a lasting impact on how complicated subjects might be handled on television.

Musical Contributions

Pryor's cultural impact permeated the music business as well. Many hip-hop artists have used his storytelling style and the rhythmic cadence of his jokes as inspiration for their lyrical substance. Rappers Tupac Shakur, Eminem, and Kendrick

Lamar have all recognized the influence Pryor had on their music, pointing out how his capacity to communicate important truths from an African American viewpoint influenced the stories they told in their songs. Pryor's records, which often combine comedy and true tales, are regarded as forerunners of many contemporary hip-hop albums that include humor, social criticism, and storytelling.

Honors and Occasions in Popular Culture

Pryor has been honored in a variety of ways in pop culture as a cultural icon. Documentaries, biographies, and tributes showcasing his brilliance and cultural influence have been written about him. Comedians and actors have congregated for events like Comedy Central's "Richard Pryor Tribute" night when they discuss Pryor's impact on their careers and the entertainment business.

Numerous accolades, including an Emmy and five Grammy Awards, have been given to him in recognition of his ground-breaking approach to humor and the boundaries he broke down. His recognition as a key figure in American culture is further cemented by his admission into the Hollywood Walk of Fame and his receipt of the Mark Twain Prize for American Humor.

Final Thoughts

Finally, This section captures the essence of how Richard Pryor evolved from a stand-up comedian to a multidimensional representation of cultural advancement. He is a timeless emblem of artistic boldness and honesty because of his daring comedy that tackles social concerns, his groundbreaking work in cinema and television, and his enduring impact on music and popular culture. Pryor's status as an American legend is assured by his legacy as a cultural icon, which continues to inspire and impact upcoming performers and artists.

Chapter 5

An Analytical Examination of Pryor's Most Distinguished Performances

Richard Pryor's body of work is examined in depth in this section which includes several critical pieces analyzing his most well-known stand-up routines and film appearances. This section explores the persistent elements of Pryor's performances that continue to have an impact on audiences even decades after they were first performed, in addition to honoring his brilliance. This analysis explores the subtleties that make Pryor's work both ground-breaking and ageless, giving us insight into his significant effect on comedy and society.

The 1976 film "Silver Streak"

Essays center on Pryor's portrayal as Grover Muldoon in "Silver Streak," his collaboration with

Gene Wilder, which allowed him to quietly address racial prejudices while showcasing a keen sense of comic timing. This performance is renowned for its unique fusion of humor, action, and racial criticism, demonstrating Pryor's ability to subvert social standards with laughter.

The 1980 song "Stir Crazy"

Another hit partnership between Pryor and Wilder, "Stir Crazy" showcased Pryor's comic brilliance in a mainstream context and went on to become one of the year's biggest earning movies. This section's critics discuss how Pryor's interpretation of Skip Donahue gave a complex dimension to a character that might have been a straight comedy, and they provide a compelling argument for the significance of Black protagonists in Hollywood comedies.

Critical Approval and Heritage

These studies also look at how Pryor's works were received critically at their first release and how that opinion has changed over time. They talk about how comedy has evolved along with society's standards and preferences, taking into account how Pryor's sometimes provocative material has endured the test of time. The articles also examine the wider effects of Pryor's impact on succeeding generations of comedians and filmmakers, pointing out how his unafraid approach to humor and his readiness to tackle tough subjects cleared the way for more candid conversations in popular media.

Final Thoughts

In addition to honoring Richard Pryor's talent as a performer, "A Critical Look at Pryor's Most Memorable Performances" provides a critical perspective on his work, shedding light on its intricacy and cultural relevance. This section analyzes these performances to highlight the layers of truth, sorrow, and comedy that characterize Pryor's legacy as a comic and as a key player in the development of American entertainment. This analytical examination contributes to solidifying Pryor's reputation as a revolutionary artist whose creations never cease to excite and impact others.

Pryor's Narrative Method

The approach used by Richard Pryor is a distinct storytelling approach emphasizing how his storytelling revolutionized stand-up comedy and impacted other entertainment genres. Pryor's narrative stood out for its unadulterated emotional depth, sharp social critique, and deftly blending tragedy with comedy, which gave viewers a humorous perspective on weighty subjects.

Pryor's Narrative Style's Foundations
Richard Pryor's storytelling style was strongly influenced by his own experiences as a difficult-to-grow child raised in a Peoria, Illinois, brothel. Pryor's performances vividly described the

complex tapestry of persons, locales, and events that these encounters afforded. His autobiographical narrative style allowed him to explore universal issues of sorrow, pleasure, love, and social injustice while also establishing a personal connection with his audience.

Methods and Presentation

Pryor's storytelling approach was characterized by many essential methods which includes:

- Characterization: Pryor was an expert at creating several personas with his voice and physique, from a tired elderly man to an inquisitive youngster. His ability to change characters without breaking the storyline helped him to explore a variety of viewpoints and make his works more relatable.

- Dialogue and Dialects: He enhanced the realism of his tales by deftly using a variety of dialects and accents to give his characters life. His ability to imitate speech patterns enhanced the comedy's narrative setting by evoking socioeconomic and geographical backgrounds.

- Emotional Layering: Reflecting the intricacies of actual life, Pryor imbued his stories with a complex layering of emotions, often shifting quickly from laughter to melancholy or rage. Because of its emotional depth and realistic portrayal of human experience, his humor had a profound emotional resonance.

- Pacing and time: He had a superb sense of time and knew just how to pace his storytelling to fascinate people. Pryor often built suspense and then broke it with a sudden change to a hilarious or ludicrous aspect. He also understood whether to dwell on a joke or go straight to the punchline.

Social Commentary via Narrative

Pryor made social commentary via narrative, focusing on themes of racism and injustice, in addition to providing entertainment. He addressed these issues head-on, but instead of preaching outright, he used stories to gently highlight the inequities and absurdities in society. His account of a family outing to the zoo, for instance, gently criticized racial and social dynamics by imitating the responses of various animals to the presence of a black man.

Impact on Different Media

Beyond stand-up comedy, Pryor had a significant narrative impact on cinema and television, where he often contributed to character development and screenplays. A generation of comedians and filmmakers that aimed to more subtly and meaningfully weave social issues into their works were impacted by his storytelling technique.

Legacy

Many modern comedians and storytellers who credit Richard Pryor as a key inspiration bear witness to the impact of Pryor's storytelling method. Following in Pryor's footsteps, comedians like Eddie Murphy, Dave Chappelle, and Chris Rock use narrative comedy to address difficult societal topics in a way that strikes a balance between humor and seriousness.

Final Thoughts

In summary, we emphasize how Richard Pryor's storytelling transformed stand-up comedy into an expressive art form. Pryor educated and thrilled his audiences by fusing personal tales with more general societal criticism, which forced them to consider the society in which they lived. His storytelling technique is still regarded as the best in comedy, valued for its profundity, originality, and potency.

Pryor's Legacy in Today's Comedy Scene

Pryor has had a lasting influence on comedy and it will continue to inspire generations to come. His singular fusion of unadulterated honesty, intense emotional nuance, and daring social problem confrontation raised the bar for what comedy was capable of. This section highlights the enduring effect of Pryor's legacy by examining how his work permeates the work of modern comedians on a variety of mediums, including stand-up, television, and cinema.

The genre of stand-up comedy was revolutionized by Richard Pryor's witty and insightful social satire and introspective honesty. He invented a new kind of humorous expression that aimed to provoke thought in addition to laughter. Pryor's skill at delving into social and personal suffering while maintaining elegance and comedy made it possible for comedians to tackle heavier, sometimes taboo subjects in their performances.

Comedians such as Eddie Murphy, Chris Rock, and Dave Chappelle, who have all recognized Pryor as a significant influence on their careers, showcase Pryor's impact on stand-up. These comedians have tackled difficult subjects like racism, injustice, and personal struggle using their platforms.

Dave Chappelle often credits Pryor as his biggest inspiration, drawing parallels between Pryor's ability to combine comedy with astute insights about race and culture. Pryor's influence may be seen in Chappelle's stand-up specials, such as *Killing Them Softly* and his more recent *Sticks & Stones*, which have a strong social criticism and narrative structure.

Chris Rock has picked up Pryor's mantle of confronting societal problems head-on, especially those about relationships and race. Rock's comic routines, like those in *Bring the Pain* and *Bigger & Blacker*, clearly trace back to Pryor.

Cinema and TV

Pryor's influence is seen in cinema and television, as a new wave of humorous storytelling has been shaped by his narrative style and daring conceptual choices. Pryor's influence may be seen in television programs like Donald Glover's *Atlanta* and Aziz Ansari's *Master of None*, which combine humor and drama to tackle social problems impactfully and subtly.

- **Donald Glover's** "Atlanta" echoes Pryor's ability to make surprising observations on race and social concerns by fusing profound comments on the African American experience with surreal comedy.
- **Jordan Peele** has made the switch from comedy to horror with movies like *Get Out* and *Us*, but he keeps Pryor's legacy alive by using entertaining social criticism. Peele's examination of race and

culture, pushing limits and confronting audiences, is a reflection of Pryor's legacy.

Writing and Acting Comedies
Pryor also influenced contemporary comedians' writing and acting styles. His unwavering honesty and profound emotional range have inspired other comedians to divulge more intimate and exposed parts of their lives in their performances, turning stand-up into a platform for both social criticism and individual expression.

The Wider Legacy of Pryor
Beyond specific performances, the legacy of Richard Pryor lies in the philosophy he introduced to comedy: a philosophy that values the audience's intellect and acknowledges that laughter cannot only relieve pain but also stimulate thinking. His impact may be seen in the growing number of comedians who don't mind challenging their

audiences with challenging personal or political content or speaking truth to power.

Final Thoughts

Finally, Richard Pryor's groundbreaking style of humor has influenced the genre's current state. Numerous comedians who strive to engage audiences in ways that go beyond simple humor—in addition to providing entertainment—have carried on his legacy via their work. Because of his work, Pryor has raised the bar for what comedy can achieve, cementing his legacy as an iconic figure whose influence is still felt in the comic community today in fresh and changing forms.

Pryor's Influence on the Dramatic Arts

This section explores the significant ways that Richard Pryor has impacted dramatic narrative both within and outside of the comedy genre. Pryor is most known for his groundbreaking stand-up comedy, but his work also included dramatic elements, demonstrating his flexibility and significant influence on the dramatic arts. This examination looks at the lasting influence he has had on theater via his representation of characters, depth of story, and emotional resonance.

Dramatic Roles for Pryor

Richard Pryor's entry into the world of serious acting offered spectators a fresh perspective on his abilities. In movies like "Blue Collar" (1978) and "Lady Sings the Blues" (1972), Pryor showed that he could play sensitive and nuanced parts. He portrayed a desperate auto worker entangled in a web of union corruption and personal strife in

"Blue Collar," a role that is often praised for its unadulterated sincerity and emotional depth. Diana Ross's Billie Holiday was enhanced by Pryor's nuanced depiction of Piano Man in "Lady Sings the Blues," which combined comedy and a moving emotional presence.

Impact on Dramatic Presentation

Pryor's experience in stand-up comedy, where character authenticity, emotional expression, and narrative are crucial, greatly impacted his approach to his dramatic parts. His ability to emote complexly and draw from personal experience gave his dramatic characters depth, which made him an engaging actor in both serious and humorous parts. He often portrayed layers of sensitivity, rage, and vulnerability in his performances, giving viewers a complex understanding of his characters that struck a profound chord.

Effect on Directing and Screenwriting

Pryor's influence on the dramatic arts also extended to screenplay and directing, two fields in which his ability to tell stories was essential. His writings often combined drama and comedy, demonstrating his keen awareness of the complexity of human existence. One semi-autobiographical film that Pryor directed and wrote the screenplay for, "Jo Jo Dancer, Your Life Is Calling," for example, demonstrates his skill at fusing comedy with weighty subjects like addiction and self-redemption. This movie serves as an example of how Pryor's storytelling abilities might go beyond traditional genre constraints to provide a more in-depth examination of character and plot.

Legacy in Modern Drama

The work of modern performers and directors, who combine humor and drama to explore intricate societal and personal subjects, is influenced by Pryor. Following in Pryor's footsteps, performers like Jamie Foxx and Robin Williams and filmmakers like Jordan Peele and Spike Lee have used their platforms to tackle important subjects through a lens that combines tragic and humorous aspects. Because of Pryor's skill at balancing humor and seriousness while addressing heavy themes, the genre has become more fluid, blurring the boundaries between comedy and drama to provide deeper, more varied stories.

The Impact of Education
Pryor's efforts have also affected performing arts education, namely on writing and acting curricula. His plays and performances are often studied in drama schools and university programs as examples of how authors and performers may successfully communicate social critique, emotional depth, and sincerity. His art serves as a teaching tool for students, emphasizing the transformation of personal experiences into powerful art via the force of honesty and vulnerability in performance.

Conclusively, The important but often disregarded contributions Richard Pryor made to the theater are highlighted above. His work questioned genre norms, demonstrated the emotional range of humorous performers in dramatic parts, and impacted the narrative strategies used by artists in subsequent generations. In addition to confirming his status as a comic genius, Pryor's impact on the dramatic arts demonstrates his flexibility as an artist and his deep comprehension of the human condition. He also plays a crucial role in the wider realm of contemporary entertainment.

Chapter 6

Relationships and Marital life of Richard Pryor

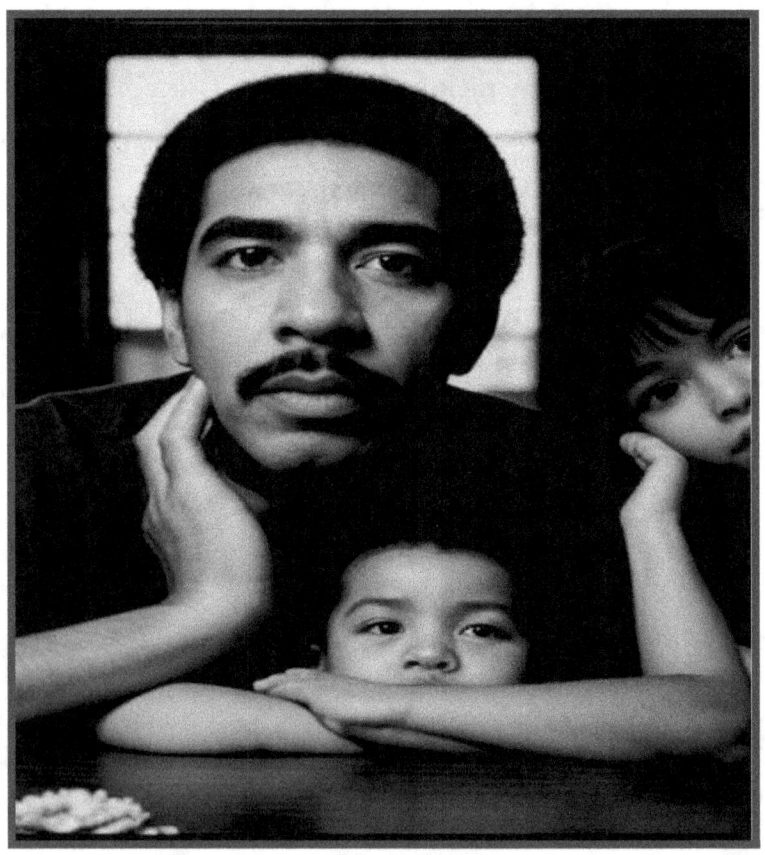

The comedian Richard Pryor's marriage and relationships were equally complicated and turbulent. His several marriages, close relationships, and the challenges and insights they brought about shaped his personal life throughout the years and often inspired his comedic works. We shall discuss his marital journey below;

Richard Pryor wed five different ladies on seven separate occasions:

1. Patricia Price (1960–1961) :– Pryor's first marriage lasted just a year before terminating in divorce. Richard Pryor Jr. is Pryor's first kid from this relationship.

2. Shelly Bonis (1967–1969) :– Pryor's second marriage, which was also brief, terminated partly as a result of his issues with drug addiction and growing demands from his work.

3. Deborah McGuire (1977–1978) :– Pryor wed the actress and model in a well-reported ceremony.

Their marriage, which was characterized by a prominent lifestyle and many public appearances, terminated abruptly, mostly as a result of Pryor's growing drug abuse and the instability in their union.

4. Jennifer Lee (1979–1982; 2001–2005) :– Pryor had two wives, Jennifer Lee being his fourth and seventh. They were married for the first time in 1979 and again in 2001. Pryor's health issues were mostly managed by Jennifer, particularly after his 1986 multiple sclerosis diagnosis. In addition, she took great care of him and oversaw his legacy after his passing.

5. Pryor twice married and divorced Flynn Belaine (1986–1987; 1990–1991). Together, they were parents to two kids. Several public and private difficulties that were often made worse by Pryor's health problems and his ongoing drug usage characterized their partnership.

Relationship Dynamics: Pryor's relationships were often troubled and quite visible at the same time. His marriages and relationships were dynamic and sometimes turbulent due to his battles with addiction and his complicated nature. His marital struggles regularly served as the basis for his stand-up performances, in which he drew humor from his personal life that was frank and sometimes brutally honest, and which audiences found relatable and real.

Relationships' Effect on His Career: Relationships had a big effect on Pryor's emotional and mental health, which affected his performances and the stages of his career. His marriages, especially the one he had with Jennifer Lee in his latter years were very important to his career's upswing and downswing, especially during his fight with multiple sclerosis.

Comedy as a Mirror: During his stand-up routine, Pryor was candid about his relationship setbacks and struggles, often blending comedy and sadness in his remarks. Audiences that valued both his humor and his ability to face up to his shortcomings found resonance in his comedy when he was open about his marital issues and thoughtful about his shortcomings.

Final Thoughts: The passion, strife, and tenderness that characterized Richard Pryor's marriage and relationships reflected the extremes of his public image. His life and writings were shaped by each relationship, which illustrated the difficulties associated with love, devotion, and personal development. His candid discussion of his personal experiences shaped the confessional comedy approach that many other comedians have adopted.

Pryor as a Social Commentator

"Pryor as a Social Commentator" examines how Richard Pryor deftly used activism and humor to address important racial, socioeconomic, and social norms problems using his stand-up comedy as a platform. This section explores Pryor's capacity to draw attention to the shortcomings and inequities in society, which makes him a powerful advocate for change and a spark for conversations on a range of social issues.

Addressing Racial Concerns

Pryor's comedic approach to confronting race and prejudice in America was one of its most important features. He approached the subject with fearlessness. He engaged his audience with a combination of deep truths and witty repartee, never holding back when exposing the injustices and absurdities of racial prejudice. His routines often shed light on African Americans' daily lives, offering a sharp contrast to the frequently sanitized narratives that are widely accepted in the media. His views on racial profiling, police brutality, and the differences in how the judicial system treats people struck a chord with many people who had firsthand experience with these realities, for example and went beyond humorous sketches to become insightful commentary.

Economic Inequality and Class

Pryor's comedy also touched on issues of economic injustice and class conflict. He was frank in his discussion of the difficulties associated with poverty and the difficulties of upward mobility in a class-based society. His sketches often showed people who were having a hard time making ends meet, showing the human aspect of financial problems. His viewers were forced to consider the underlying social and economic systems as a result of the humor as well as the way it brought attention to larger societal problems that led to these situations.

Intimidating Social Norms

Pryor's humor often questioned a range of social conventions, including those about gender, sexuality, and addiction, in addition to race and class. His candor about his personal experiences—such as his battles with drug addiction and his thoughts on sexual politics—pushed the bounds of what was considered appropriate conversation. This transparency promoted more honest dialogue among the general population and assisted in de-stigmatizing these problems.

Worldwide Applicability and Durability

Notable are Pryor's influence as a social analyst and his worldwide reach. He became a global celebrity in both entertainment and activism because of his comedy albums and concert videos, which also helped promote his views. Because of the universal issues in his work and the distinctive way he delivered it, audiences throughout the world were able to relate to his critique of American culture and find similarities in their own local experiences.

However, His stand-up was not just about making people laugh; it was also about making people think, questioning social standards, and starting conversations that went far beyond comedy clubs and theaters. In addition to his comedic legacy, Pryor is regarded as one of the most prominent social commentators of his day, highlighting and addressing important concerns of the day with humor.

The Last Draw

We'll take a thoughtful look at Richard Pryor's last years, his death, and the lingering legacy that honors his enormous contributions to popular culture and entertainment. This was the height of his successful career as well as a moment of major personal difficulties.

Death : At the age of 65, Richard Pryor departed from this life on December 10, 2005. His continual health problems culminated in a heart attack that claimed his life. His death sparked intense sadness among admirers all across the globe and in the entertainment business, underscoring the close bond he had developed with viewers via his career and personal hardships.

Legacy and Posthumous Recognition

Richard Pryor's contributions to comedy and the larger cultural landscape have come to be appreciated and honored more and more in the years after his passing. Numerous tributes and retrospectives have emphasized his breakthrough impact on stand-up comedy as well as his innovative use of humor to address social concerns.

Honors and Awards

Pryor's influence on the entertainment business is evident in the many posthumous awards he has been bestowed with. Notably, in 1998 he received the first Kennedy Center Mark Twain Prize for American Humor, which acknowledged his great impact as a humorist and social critic. In addition, in 2006, "Richard Pryor: Live in Concert," a legendary concert film, was inducted into the National Film Registry, guaranteeing that his legacy would go on for a long time as a part of American culture.

Impact on Next Generations

The themes and style of Richard Pryor are still relevant and have an impact on upcoming comics and performers. His distinctive storytelling style, sharp social critique, and unwavering honesty have made him a global inspiration for comedians and entertainers. Comedians such as Eddie Murphy, Chris Rock, and Dave Chappelle have all acknowledged Pryor as having had a significant impact on their careers and have often adopted his style of fusing comedy with moving social criticism.

Remembering and Ongoing Festivities

Pryor has continued to be honored by a variety of media, such as documentaries, biographies, and special features that delve into his life and legacy. These homages not only honor his accomplishments but also provide fresh perspectives on his personal and professional setbacks, underscoring his enormous influence on his contemporaries and audience.

Moral and Life Lessons from the Story of Richard Pryor

Those who are acquainted with Richard Pryor's journey will find great resonance in the multitude of moral and life lessons contained in his life tale, which is characterized by both spectacular highs and devastating lows. From his modest beginnings in a Peoria, Illinois, brothel, to rising to the pinnacle of comedic stardom, and enduring personal crises and health problems, Pryor's life was a complicated tapestry that offers important lessons about fortitude, sincerity, and the capacity for change.

1.) Vulnerability and Authenticity: The importance of being genuine and vulnerable is among the most important lessons to be learned from Pryor's life. By bringing a raw honesty to stand-up comedy and often touching on taboo subjects like his background, addiction, and personal failings, Pryor revolutionized the genre. His genuineness not only made him stand out in the comedy industry but also imparted to viewers the value of accepting one's truth, no matter how flawed. Pryor inspired people to live authentically and without pretense by demonstrating that vulnerability can be a virtue rather than a weakness.

2.) Accomplishment Despite Difficulties: Pryor had several obstacles throughout his life, including fighting multiple sclerosis later in life and growing up in an abusive and difficult home. His incredible tenacity was shown by his ability to face these obstacles head-on and turn them into content for his humor. Adversity may be a source of strength and progress, he imparted to his audience. His fortitude offers guidance on how to face life's setbacks with dignity and wit, turning personal adversity into a source of wisdom and mirth.

3.) The Creative Process's Redemptive Power: One of the main themes of Pryor's life and work was creativity as a means of atonement. Comedy provided him both a haven and a platform for atonement throughout his turbulent life. Pryor utilized his artistic abilities to manage and make sense of his circumstances, whether he was facing personal demons, public controversies, or health issues. This element of his life serves as a striking example of the redeeming power of creativity, showing how it can be used to heal, give voice to the voiceless, and affect societal and personal transformation.

4.) Social Inquiry and Accountability: Pryor's writings did not hold back when confronting societal injustices, particularly those about inequality and racism. He made his listeners laugh while exposing the injustices and absurdities of society's standards and provoking thought. His bravery in taking on these problems head-on shows how artists must utilize their platforms for social criticism. Comedy and entertainment can be more than simply a means of escape; Pryor's legacy shows that they can also act as catalysts for societal awareness and change.

5.) The Value of Individual Growth: Pryor saw tremendous personal changes throughout his life, from honing his humorous approach to kicking addiction and adopting a more contemplative way of living in his final years. His experience serves as a reminder of the value of ongoing personal growth and development. Pryor's readiness to adapt and develop—often in the spotlight—is evidence of the never-ending quest for self-awareness and the bravery required to change with time.

6.) Accepting Innovation and Change: Richard Pryor's career was distinguished by his ability to adjust to the times, modifying his subject and manner to mirror his development as well as societal shifts. By incorporating personal anecdotes, he redefined stand-up comedy, turning conventional setups into a more impromptu and emotionally charged performance. The importance of creativity and adaptation in any industry is shown by his readiness to accept change and push the limits of his art form. Pryor's example shows us that taking chances and accepting change may result in ground-breaking accomplishments.

7.) Transparency's Effect on Relationships: Pryor's openness in his work life was a reflection of his relationships with others. Through candidly sharing his shortcomings and difficulties, Pryor cultivated stronger relationships with both his audience and others in his vicinity. Establishing trust and understanding in both personal and professional relationships may be greatly aided by this degree of openness. Pryor's story demonstrates how being truthful and forthright might make one vulnerable, but it can also foster deeper, more genuine relationships.

8.) Humor's Healing Power: Throughout his battles with addiction, medical conditions, and inner anguish, Pryor used comedy as a therapeutic technique in addition to a coping method. By allowing himself to laugh at his lowest points, he not only helped himself manage but also allowed others to laugh at their struggles, which eased their load. Pryor's use of humor highlights its healing potential and implies that finding the funny amid hardship may be a useful strategy for reducing stress and suffering.

9.) Confronting Your Demons: Richard Pryor battled several demons throughout his life, including drug misuse and issues arising from his background. His readiness to take on these challenges head-on in both his private and public life serves as a potent example of bravery and the value of owning up to one's troubles. This conversation is essential for growth and development as well as for personal healing. Pryor showed how confronting personal concerns may result in genuine transformation and healing, while avoiding or denying them just makes them worse.

10.) Creating Legacy Via Honesty: Pryor never wavered in his dedication to being true to himself, even in the face of many obstacles. In the highly commercialized entertainment sector, where artists are often under pressure to meet popular expectations, he maintained his integrity. Because of his sincerity, he was able to leave behind a lasting legacy that was founded on his genuine creative vision and values. Pryor's career serves as an example of how adhering to one's principles and ideals may inspire others and have a long-lasting effect in addition to helping to create a real personal and professional identity.

In summary, The moral and life lessons imparted by Richard Pryor's narrative transcend well beyond the realm of humor. His life serves as an example of the value of being true to oneself, the strength that comes from showing vulnerability, the healing potential of art, the significance of social duty, and the ongoing nature of human growth. These insights turn Pryor's story into something both captivating and very educational, offering timeless knowledge that inspires and influences others long after his death.

Richard Pryor left behind an enduring legacy that will always shine a light on comedy and other fields for the next generations. His life and work are timeless sources of inspiration because they show that anybody can have a significant impact on culture and society if they possess bravery, sincerity, and a deep grasp of human nature. Going ahead, it is certain that Richard Pryor's impact will endure, serving as a source of guidance and inspiration for not just comedians but also for anybody aspiring to question the existing quo and effect change via their artistic endeavors.

Happy Reading....

www.ingramcontent.com/pod-product-compliance
Lightning Source LLC
Chambersburg PA
CBHW050110230526
45470CB00004B/1756